SWU-NAP- 009

UNIFORMS OF RUSSIAN ARMY DURING THE NAPOLEONIC WAR VOL.4

UNDER THE REIGN OF PAUL I
EMPEROR OF RUSSIA BETWEEN 1796 AND 1801
ARTILLERY, ENGINEERS, AND GARRISONS 1796-1801

From the Viskovatov's greatest work:
"Historical description of the clothing and
arms of the Russian Army"

English translation by Mark Conrad

SOLDIER.SHOP PUBLISHING

AUTHOR

Aleksandr Vasilevich Viskovatov born 22 April (4 May New Style) 1804, died 27 February (11 March) 1858 in St. Petersburg, Russian military historian. He graduated from the 1st Cadet Corps and served in the artillery, the hydrographic depot of the Naval Ministry, and then in the Department of Military Educational Institutions. He mainly studied historical artifacts and the histories of military units. Viskovatov's greatest work was the Historical Description of the Clothing and Arms of the Russian Army.

TRANSLATOR

Mark Conrad is an American historian with a great interest for all the Russian history.

Title: **UNIFORMS OF RUSSIAN ARMY DURING THE NAPOLEONIC WAR VOL. 4 -**
Artillery, Engineers, and Garrisons 1796-1801
By A.V. Viskovatov. English translation by Mark Conrad. First edition by Soldiershop.
Cover & Art Design: Luca S. Cristini. Plates re-colorations by Anna Cristini
ISBN code: 978-88-93270410

Published by Soldiershop publishing, via Padre Davide, 7 - 24050 Zanica (BG) ITALY. www.soldiershop.com

UNIFORMS
OF THE RUSSIAN
ARMY DURING THE
NAPOLEONIC WAR VOL.4

UNDER THE REIGN OF PAUL I EMPEROR OF
RUSSIA BETWEEN 1796 AND 1801

*

Artillery, Engineers, and Garrisons 1796-1801

HISTORICAL DESCRIPTION OF THE CLOTHING AND ARMS
OF THE RUSSIAN ARMY - A.V. VISKOVATOV
(First English translation by Mark Conrad)

Soldiershop is glad to presents the complete collection of the great job made by A.V. Viskovatov dedicated to the uniforms and weapons belonging to the Russian army during the Napoleonic period, until 1825. The time we considered corresponds to the reigns of two Tzars: Paul I, who reigned since 1769 until his murder on the 23rd of March 1801, and his son Aleksandr Pavlovi☐ Romanov, that with the title of Alexander I, sat on the throne until the 1st December 1825.

Our reprint in based on the original 19th century volumes, to be precise the volumes from 7 to 9 are dedicated to the reign of Paul I; this first part is distributed on 7 volumes, having a numbering from 1 to 7. From number 10 to 18 of the original volumes, the second part is dedicated to the Russian troops under Alexander I. These still being worked on and they will be soon ready, distributed on twenty volumes approximately. Our new edition, the first ever published in English, both on paper and digital format, boasts a large number of color plates, many of them unpublished and coloured by our team of expert artists and scholars of uniformology. Each volume is based on 50/70 plates, always accompanied by the original translated text which describes the uniforms, the organization and the armament of the Russian army of the period.

A unique work in its genre, a must have in any respecting collection!

Aleksandr Vasilevich Viskovatov born 22 April (4 May New Style) 1804, died 27 February (11 March) 1858 in St. Petersburg, Russian military historian. He graduated from the 1st Cadet Corps and served in the artillery, the hydrographic depot of the Naval Ministry, and then in the Department of Military Educational Institutions.

He mainly studied historical artifacts and the histories of military units. Viskovatov's greatest work was the Historical Description of the Clothing and Arms of the Russian Army (Vols. 1-30, St. Petersburg, 1841-62; 2nd ed. Vols. 1-34, St. Petersburg - Novosibirsk - Leningrad, 1899-1948). This work is based on a great quantity of archival documents and contains four thousand colored illustrations.

Viskovatov was the author of Chronicles of the Russian Army (Books 1-20, St. Petersburg, 1834-42) and Chronicles of the Russian Imperial Army (Parts 1-7, St. Petersburg, 1852). He collected valuable material on the history of the Russian navy which went into A Short Overview of Russian Naval Campaigns and General Voyages to the End of the XVII Century (St. Petersburg, 1864; 2nd edition Moscow, 1946). Together with A.I. Mikhailovskii-Danilevskii he helped prepare and create the Military Gallery in the Winter Palace.

He wrote the historical military inscriptions for the walls of the Hall of St. George in the Great Palace of the Kremlin. (From the article in the Soviet Military Encyclopedia.)

CONTENTS

*

Preface pag. 5

*

Russian Army: Artillery, Engineers,
and Garrisons 1796-1801 pag. 7

VII Artillery pag. 7
VIII. Corps of Engineers pag. 11
IX. Garrisons   pag. 13

*

Notes pag. 29

*

Plates pag. 35

RUSSIAN ARMY,

Artillery, Engineers, and Garrisons 1796-1801

Changes in the uniforms and equipment of Army Cavalry, Artillery, Engineers, and Garrisons, from 1796 to 1801

VII.   Artillery
VIII. Corps of Engineers
IX.   Garrisons

VII. ARTILLERY (Artilleriya)

Upon EMPEROR PAUL I's ascension to the Throne, Army Artillery (divided into Siege, Field, and Horse) received the same uniforms and arms as the Artillery of the Gatchina troops. At first all changes in these units were done, with HIGHEST permission, by Artillery command itself and later fully entered into tables confirmed by HIGHEST authority on 12 March 1798.

Based on the tables and preceding changes, privates , i.e. bombardiers, cannoneers, and gun handlers (bombardiry, kanoniry i gandlangery) of the Siege (Osadnaya) as well as the Field Artillery (Polevaya Artilleriya), were given a dark-green kaftan coat, without lapels, with as very low standing collar of the same color. The coat had dark-green round cuffs edged, as were the cuff flaps, with red cloth piping; a rend cloth strap on the left shoulder; red kersey lining and flat brass buttons. With this were prescribed: waistcoat and breeches of straw-colored cloth and gaiters of black cloth, all three with brass buttons. For summer there were white breeches of Flemish linen. Greased shoes with blunt toes; red stamin neck cloth with white tape edging and a similar tapes in the back to tie it with; three-cornered hat with white edging, tied with a black woolen cord, brass button and three woolen tassels colored red; dark-green cloth forage cap with or without a band; white cloth cloak with or without a hood (capishon). For winter, a sheepskin warm coat (fufaika). Weapons and accouterments consisted of the theshort sword (tesak) prescribed for grenadiers and musketeers, with asword knot with the same different colors as for those regiments; a standard infantry swordbelt; powder flask (porokhovaya natruska) with a whitened cross belt worn over the left shoulder (Illus. 1059); knapsack; water flask; and rusk bag. In the Field Artillery, a horse's authorized price was 30 roubles (156).

Fireworkers (feierverkery, i.e. non-commissioned officers) and officer candidates (yunkera) were dinstinguished as non-commissioned officers in infantry regiments with gold galloon on cuffs, cuff flaps, and hat; a mix of orange and black silk in the tassels on the hat and sword knot; gloves the same color as the waistcoat; and a cane. Weapons and accouterments for them were all the same as for bombardiers, cannoneers, and gun handlers except for the powder flask, which they were not authorized (Illus. 1059) (157).

Company drummers—a strap on the right shoulder; dark-green wings with red piping and four sewn-on stripes on each sleeve, of white tape with thin black stripes and red and yellow worms (zmeiki, zigzag lines). Artillery drums had frames or hoops with triangles in two colors: dark green and white. Drum sticks were straw colored (Illus. 1060) (158).

Battalion drummers, and when battalions were combined into regiments—regimental drummers, had in addition to stripes sewn onto the sleeves similar tape on all seams of the coat and all the same distinctions as prescribed for fireworkers and officer candidates (Illus. 1060) (159).

Officers had: kaftan coat, the same as for lower ranks except with convex gilt buttons; straw-colored waistcoat with wide gold galloon; straw-colored breeches; white neck cloth; hat with narrow gold galloon; gaiters;boots; gloves (the same color as the waistcoat); cane; sword (shpaga) with swordknot and sash—all the same as for officers in infantry regiments (Illus. 1061). Field-grade officers wore boots with spurs and had the skirts of their coats turned back (160).

Generals were distinguished from field-grade officers only by their wide galloon and—on the hat—a cockade of black ribbon with orange checks, gold buttonhole loop, and white plumage (161).

Train personnel (furshtatskie) and other non-combatant lower ranks such as: junior train-masters (unter-furmeistery), farriers (konovaly), saddlers (sedel'nyi i shornyi), gun-stock maker (lozhennyi); smith (kuznechnyi), journeyman metal worker (slesarnyi podmaster), their apprentices, solderer (payal'shchik), carpenters (plotniki), wheelwrights (kolesniki), turners (tokari), joiners (stolyary), train personnel (furleity), and provost (profos), were uninformed following the example of non-combatant ranks in Army infantry regiments. Only junior train-masters had frock coats (sertuki) with gold galloon on the cuffs and cuff flaps, big cavalry boots with bell tops and iron spurs, white gloves, and a cane (Illus. 1062) (162). Train personnel wore the same boots and were authorized, just as were junior train-masters, white cloth valises for riding on horseback (163).

Train officers (furshtatskie ofitsery), namely: Train Masters (Furmeistery), Junior Forage Master (Unter-Furazhmeister), Forage Master (Furazhmeister), and Supply Train Chief (Oboznyi), as well as the Quartermaster (Kvartirmister) and Auditor (Auditor), all had uniforms following the pattern for Quartermasters and Auditors, while the Doctor (Lekar') followed the example of Doctors in Army regiments (164).

Bombardiers and cannoneers of the Horse Artillery (Konnaya Artillery) had: kaftan coat and waistcoat, identical to those in the foot Artillery except that the first had the skirts turned back;breeches of white cloth and another pair, for summer, of Flemish linen; boots with blunt toes, bell tops, iron spurs, and gaiter cuffs; black clothneck cloth; hat like that for foot artillery; gloves the same straw color as the waistcoat;forage cap of dark-green cloth, with or without a cap band; cloak of white cloth with or without a hood; dragoon broadsword (palash) with an infantry sword knot colored by company, dragoon sword belt and pistol on a white crossbelt with an iron hook, worn over the left shoulder. Additionally, each man was prescribed: knapsack with water flask and rusk bag. Horse furniture consisted of: dragoon saddle with all appurtenences but without holsters; shabrack of dark-green cloth with trim, monogram, and crown of straw-colored cloth (Illus. 1063), and valise, sack, and bag all of the patterns for cuirassiers and dragoons (165). Horse-artillery horses were prescribed to cost 60 roubles (166).

Fireworkers and officer candidates had gold galloon on cuffs, cuff flaps, and hats; tassels on the hat and sword knot had black and orange silk; cane; two pistols secured in holsters in which were places for cartridges, and dark-green cloth pistol holders with the same straw-colored trim, monogram, and crown as for bombardiers and cannoneers (Illus. 1063) (167).

Officers had a kaftan coat and waistcoat that were the same as in the foot Artillery with with turned back skirts; deerskin breeches; boots with bell tops, spurs, and gaiter cuffs; black neck cloth; hat with narrow gold galloon; gloves the same color as the waistcoat; sword (shpaga) identical to the one cuirassier officers wore with the undress coat; sash and cane. In mounted order they had two pistols, a saddle with all its appurtenences, and—of dark-green cloth with gold galloon and similar monograms and crowns—shabrack and pistol holders (Illus. 1064) (168).

Generals, just as in the foot Artillery, wore hats with wide galloon, a cockade, buttonhole loop, and plumage (169).

Train personnel and all other non-combatant ranks were the same as in the foot Artillery with the sole addition of a Stablemaster (Shtalmeister), and were uniformed the same as non-combatants—and the Stablemaster, as Stablemasters—in Cavalry regiments (170).

Musicians, eight in number and authorized only for the senior siege battalion, were uniformed and armed following the example of foot Artillery fireworkders and officer candidates, with the only change being that instead of breeches, gaiters, and shoes, they had jäger chakchiry pants and boots and a belt or sash of hussar pattern made from straw-colored cord with green bindings and two likewise green cords (Illus. 1065) (171).

In Artillery commands (Artilleriiskiya komandy) in Grenadier and Musketeer regiments, bombardiers, cannoneers, fireworkers, officer candidates, officers, and non-combatants (e.g. junior train-masters, medics (fel'dshera), and train personnel—had uniforms, weapons, and accouterments the same as their corresponding ranks in foot Artillery battalions (172).

In the Pioneer Regiment that was included as part of the Artillery, private pioneers (ryadovye pionery) had uniform clothing similar to that for the foot Artillery except that the waistcoat and breeches were orange (oranzhevye); buttons (on the kaftan coat and waistcoat) were tinned white. Instead of a hat they had a leather cap (shapka) bound with orange cloth on which the frontpiece—4-1/2 vershoks (7-3/8 inches) high, band, and strips on the crown were of English iron, while the small ball at the joining of the strips was of tin (Illus. 1066 and 1067); greatcoat of dark-green cloth, with orange collar and covered buttons; and for trench work and mining operations—a smock (kitel'). Weapons and accouterments consisted of an infantry short sword (tesak) with a sword knot colored by company; an infantry sword belt without a bayonet frog; pistol kept in a white leather pistol holder (chushka) fixed to the sword belt behind the short sword; infantry cartridge box (podsumka) (Illus. 1066); knapsack, water flask, and rusk bag (173).

Non-commissioned officers and drummers of Pioneer companies were distinguished from private pioneers exactly as officer candidates and fireworkers in the foot Artillery were distinguished from bombardiers, cannoneers, and gun handlers, except that for the first the galloon was silver and gloves white (Illus. 1068), and additionally neither one nor the other were authorized smocks (174).

Sappers and miners and their non-commissioned officers and drummers differed from the corresponding pioneer ranks only in their headdress, which were like grenadier caps, 6-1/4 vershoks (10-7/8 inches) tall, with an iron front piece, band, and strips (Illus. 1069 and 1070) (175).

The regimental drummer was uniformed as the pioneer company drummers except for the prescribed rank distinctions already described above (Illus. 1071) (176).

Officers of the Pioneer Regiment differed from those in the foot Artillery only in having silver buttons and silver gallon on the hat; waistcoat and breeches were orange; gloves white (Illus. 1072) (177).

Non-combatant lower ranks: medic, lazaret attendants, turner, wheelwright, joiner, carpenter, metal worker and apprentice blacksmith, train personnel, and junior train-master—were all uniformed as their counterpart ranks in the Artillery, but with white buttons instead of yellow. However, the Quartermaster, Auditor, and Doctor were no different from those in the Artillery (178).

Pontonniers in Pontoon Depots (pontonery Pontonnykh Depo) were uniformed after the fashion of navy sailors, and wore a kind of short coat called a Dutch frock (Gollandskii bostrog), of dark green cloth with a similar low standing collar, cuffs, cuff flaps, and skirts, with brass buttons; waistcoat (with sleeves) of white cloth, with lapels of white cloth and collar and cuffs of green cloth, and with brass buttons; wide breeches orpants (bryuki), of dark-green cloth, fastened or buttoned under the knees; white (in summer—of thread cloth (nityanye), in winter—of wool) stockings; blunt-toed boots lower than where the pants are tied off; black cloth neck cloth with tape ribbons tied behind; and a Dutch hat, i.e. of black lamb's wool (poyarkovaya), with a round crown somewhat more narrow at the top, and with a narrow brim bending upwards (Illus. 1073) (179). For summer pontonneers were prescribed a waistcoat of striped ticking (of white with blue) with sleeves, cuffs, and covered buttons down the front, and white canvas (kanifasnyi) pants (Illus. 1074). While working, they wore over the waistcoat a Dutch shirt (Gollandskaya rubakha), likewise of white canvas (Illus. 1074) (180).

Non-commissioned officers in Pontoon Depots wore a dark-green cloth kaftan coat with green cloth cuffs and a low standing collar, with red kersey lining and brass buttons; white cloth waistcoat, also with brass buttons; white cloth breeches (shtany), of calamanco (kalamenko) during the summer; white stockings; short, blunt-toed boots; black neck cloth; three-cornered musketeer hat with three tassels of white, black, and orange worsted, and with narrow gold galloon; white chamois gloves; infantry short sword (tesak) with a white sword knot having an orange and black upper ring (okolysh); infantry sword belt without a bayonet frog; and a cane (Illus. 1075). Besides this every non-commissioned officer—just as the private pontooneers—were prescribed a forage cap and greatcoat, both of dark-green cloth, sheepskin fufaika coat, knapsack, water flask, and rusk bag (181).

Officers of Pontoon Depots were prescribed the exact same uniforms as officers of foot Artillery except that the waistcoat and pants were white, and instead of gaiters and shoes they wore the same boots as lower ranks (Illus. 1075) (182).

All ranks in the Artillery branches, both artillerymen themselves as well as personnel in the Pioneer Regiment and Pontoon Depots, powdered their hair and had curls and queues, while private pontooneers had only queues, without curls (183).

31 January 1799 – The white cloaks prescribed for foot and horse Artillery were replaced by dark-green greatcoats (184).

9 October 1799 – The knots (shishki) on officers' sashes, sword knots, and hat tassels, and on lower ranks' sword knots, were ordered to be colored raspberry, and stripes and tassels were to be in three colors: black, orange, and raspberry (185).

21 October 1801 – Generals and field and company-grade officers in the Artillery who wore spurs were ordered to have these in the same color as their buttons (186).

VIII. CORPS OF ENGINEERS (Inzhenernyi Korpus)

24 December 1798– Engineer personnel were ordered to have the exact same uniforms and weapons as personnel in the foot Artillery except with white buttons and silver galoon. Accountants (schetnye), ordnance personnel (tseikhdinery), wardens (vakhtery), non-commissioned officers (unter-ofitsery), and draftsmen-artists (konduktory) were uniformed as fireworkers and officer candidates; officers—as officers; and barbers and master craftsmen—as medics and master craftsmen. Doctors (lekarya) were uniformed exactly as doctors throughout the infantry (187).

26 March 1799– Engineer Arsenal Wardens and Junior Arsenal Wardens (Inzhenernye Tseikhvartery i Unter-Tseikhvartery) were ordered to have the same uniforms as infantry Quartermasters (188).

9 October 1799- The knots (shishki) on officers' sashes, sword knots, and hat tassels, and on lower ranks' sword knots, were ordered to be colored raspberry, and stripes and tassels were to be in three colors: black, orange, and raspberry (Illus. 1076) (189).

20 April 1800 – Engineer officers were given embroidered silver buttonhole loops (nashivki ili petlitsy) without small tassels, to be sewn onto the coat's collar and sleeves (190).

Saint Petersburg, Nevsky Porpesct 1800 about

IX. GARRISONS (V Garnizone)

14 November 1796– The St.-Petersburg Garrison was ordered to have the uniform of the former Gatchina battalion of Colonel Arakcheev, i.e. dark-green kaftan coat with white collar, lapels, cuffs, and shoulder strap, and with six buttonhole loops beneath the lapels, on the cuff flaps, and at the waist, of white tape with three rows of red tracery along the middle (Illus. 1077). Waistcoat and pants were white. Officers had a uniform of the same colors, but the coat did not have buttonholes (191).

Based on the Military Regulations (Voinskii Ustav) of 1796 and a HIGHEST confirmed list of colors for garrison uniforms dated 16 February 1797, Garrisons on a field establishment (Garnizony, sostoyavshie na polevom polozhenii)—which is to say St. Petersburg, Moscow, Viborg, Fredrikshamn, Reval, Riga, Archangel, Kazan, Orenburg, Smolensk, Kiev, Taganrog, Tobolsk, Selenginsk, Irkutsk, Baltic, and Dünamünde—were uniformed and armed following the example of Musketeer regiments, namely:

Musketeers had the exact same uniform and weapons as Army musketeers, except for the St.-Petersburg Garrison in which, as already stated above, buttonhole loops were not only on the cuff flaps, but also below the lapels and at the waist (Illus. 1077) (192).

Non-commissioned officers and drummers of Musketeer companies had, in addition to the same features distinguishing them from privates as existed in regiments of Army infantry, black halbard shafts and drumsticks in the two senior regiments of each division, and white ones in all the other regiments (Illus. 1078 and 1079) (193).

Privates of Grenadier companies—at first only in the Riga, Archangel, Orenburg, Selenginsk, and Kiev Garrisons, these as well as their non-commissioned officers, drummers, and fifers had, in relation to these ranks in the Musketeer companies, the same distinctions as existed in Army Musketeer regiments (Illus. 1080 and 1081) (194).

The Regimental drummer, as well as field and company-grade officers, generals, and all noncombatants, such as lazaret orderlies, medics, gun stock maker, metalsmith, gun stock and metalsmith apprentices, company master craftsmen, provosts, and—holding officer rank—the Auditor and Doctor, had uniforms as for these same ranks in the Army infantry (Illus. 1082, 1083, 1084, and 1805). For officers, spontoon shafts were black or white, corresponding to the halberds (195).

Garrisons on the internal establishment (Garnizony, na vnutrennem polozhenii), of which only the Kronstadt had Grenadier companies, were distinguished from those on a field establishment in that they had coats without buttonhole loops, lower rank hats without trim, dark-green waistcoats and pants, and for most regiments—black neck cloths (196). Privates of these Garrisons, except the Kronstadt, had swords (shpagi) with shortsword (tesachnyi) blades (Illus. 1086), bayonets instead of short swords, with the scabbards prescribed for Army grenadiers and musketeers (Illus. 1086), sword belts with frogs, and cartridge pouches without badges (197). Non-commissioned officers had galloon on the collar, cuffs, and cuff flaps; white chamois gloves, canes, swords with shortsword blades; and halberds with white shafts (Illus. 1088) (198). Drummers had sewn-on white tape with a sky-blue worm, and drum hoops that were dark green with white (Illus. 1089 and 1090). Officers wore hats with narrow galloon (Illus. 1091 and 1092) (200), while generals had wide gallon with the addition of a cockade, button loop, and plumage (Illus. 1093) (201). Non-combatant personnel, of the same positions as in Garrisons on a field establishment, differed from noncombatamts in the

Army infantry only in having dark-green pants instead of white (202).

Privates or musketeers of the Invalid companies that were part of all Garrisons, those on the internal as well as field establishment, where there were no grenadiers, had: dark-green coat, collar, cuffs, waistcoat, and pants; yellow buttons; red neck cloth; hat without trim, with three dark-green tassels. They had a sword with a shortsword blade, white sword knot, sword belt (Illus. 1094), forage cap, cloak, and warm coat—all the same as throughout the infantry (203).

Invalid non-commissioned officers were distinguished from private invalids by gold galloon on the collar, cuffs, and cuff flaps, and additionally by having the upper ring of the sword knot of black and orange worsted, gloves, and a cane (Illus. 1095) (204).

Invalid drummers had the same tape sewn onto the sleeves, and their drums the same hoops, as in combatant companies (Illus. 1096) (205).

Invalid officers wore hats with trim of narrow gold galloon, and did not have gorgets or spontoons (Illus. 1097) (206).

Invalid medics and lazaret orderlies were uniformed as these same ranks in Garrisons on the internal establishment, with the sole difference of having waistcoats with covered buttons (207).

All garrison and invalid ranks without exception used powder and wore curls and queues (208).

The colors and other distinctions established for Garrisons, with very minor changes as mentioned below, remained the same until 4 March 1800, as follows:

In the St.-Petersburg Garrison:

Lower ranks—coat with white collar, lapels, cuffs, and shoulder strap; buttonhole loops on the cuff flaps, below the lapels, and at the waist—white with red tracery, without small tassels; white waistcoat and pants; yellow buttons; red neck cloth (Illus. 1077); drum hoops dark green with white. Officers—coat without buttonhole loops; white neck cloth (209).

In the Moscow Garrison:

Lower ranks—coat with turquoise (biryuzovyi) collar, lapels, cuffs and shoulder strap; yellow buttonhole loops on the sleeves, without small tassels; white waistcoat and breeches; yellow buttons; red neck cloth (Illus. 1077); drum hoops dark-green with turqouise. Officers—gold buttonhole loops, without metallic thread (bit') or small tassels; white neck cloth (210).

In the Viborg Garrison:

Lower ranks—coat without collar or lapels, green cuffs and shoulder strap; white buttonhole loops on the sleeves, with green checks and without small tassels; white waistcoat and breeches; white buttons; red neck cloth (Illus. 1078); drum hoops dark-green with green. Officers—silver buttonhole loops on the sleeves, with checkered embroidery, of green silk, without small tassels; white neck cloth (211).

In the Fredrikshamn Garrison:

Lower ranks—coat with turquoise collar, lapels, cuffs and shoulder strap; white buttonhole loops on the sleeves, with small tassels; white waistcoat and breeches; white buttons; red neck cloth (Illus. 1078); drum hoops dark-green with turquoise. Officers—silver buttonhole loops, with small tassels, without metallic thread; white neck cloth (212).

In the Reval Garrison:

Lower ranks—coat without collar or lapels, turquoise cuffs and shoulder strap; yellow buttonhole loops on the sleeves, without small tassels; white waistcoat and breeches; yellow buttons; red neck cloth; drum hoops dark-green with turqouise (Illus. 1079). Officers—gold buttonhole loops, without small tassels, with metallic thread; white neck cloth (213).

In the Riga Garrison:
Lower ranks—coat without collar or lapels, orange cuffs and shoulder strap; yellow buttonhole loops on the sleeves, with small tassels; white waistcoat and breeches; yellow buttons; red neck cloth; orange back piece and band on the grenadier cap, with white trim (Illus. 1080); drum hoops dark-green with orange. Officers—gold buttonhole loops, with small tassels, without metallic thread; white neck cloth (214).

In the Archangel Garrison:
Lower ranks—coat with black collar, lapels, cuffs, and shoulder strap; white buttonhole loops on the sleeves, without small tassels; white waistcoat and breeches; white buttons; red neck cloth; orange back piece and band on the grenadier cap, with white trim; drum hoops dark-green with black (Illus. 1081). Officers—silver buttonhole loops, without small tassels or metallic thread; white neck cloth (215).

In the Kazan Garrison:
Lower ranks—coat with light-green collar, lapels, cuffs, and shoulder strap; yellow buttonhole loops on the sleeves, without small tassels; white waistcoat and breeches; yellow buttons; red neck cloth; drum hoops dark-green with light green (Illus. 1082). Officers—gold buttonhole loops, without small tassels; white neck cloth (216).

In the Orenburg Garrison:
Lower ranks—coat without collar or lapels, raspberry cuffs and shoulder strap; buttonhole loops on the sleeves white with raspberry edging, without small tassels; white waistcoat and breeches; white buttons; red neck cloth (Illus. 1082); orange back piece and band on the grenadier cap, with white trim (Illus. 1080); drum hoops dark-green with raspberry. Officers—buttonhole loops silver with red edging, without small tassels; white neck cloth (217).

In the Smolensk Garrison:
Lower ranks—coat with straw-colored (palevyi) collar, lapels, cuffs, and shoulder strap; yellow buttonhole loops on the sleeves, without small tassels; straw-colored waistcoat and breeches; yellow buttons; red neck cloth; drum hoops colored dark-green with straw. Officers—buttonhole loops gold, without small tassels or metallic thread; white neck cloth (Illus. 1083) (218).

In the Kiev Garrison:
Lower ranks—coat without lapels, red collar, slit cuffs and shoulder strap; white buttonhole loops on the sleeves, without small tassels; straw-colored waistcoat and breeches; white buttons; black neck cloth; orange back piece and band on the grenadier cap, with white trim; drum hoops dark-green with red. Officers—silver buttonhole loops on the cuffs, without small tassels; black neck cloth; hat with toothed wide galloon and a cockcade (Illus. 1083) (219).

In the Taganrog Garrison:
Lower ranks—coat without lapels, light sky-blue (svetlo-goluboi) collar, cuffs, and shoulder strap; white buttonhole loops on the sleeves, with small tassels; straw-colored waistcoat and breeches; white buttons; red neck cloth; drum hoops dark-green with light sky-blue. Officers—buttonhole loops on the cuffs silver with sky-blue silk, with small tassels; white neck cloth (Illus. 1083) (220).

In the Tobolsk Garrison:
Lower ranks—coat with puce (pyusovyi) collar, lapels, cuffs, and shoulder strap; white buttonhole loops on the sleeves, without small tassels; straw-colored waistcoat and breeches; white buttons; red neck cloth (Illus. 1084); drum hoops dark-green with puce. Officers—silver buttonhole loops, without small tassels, with a puce stripe; white neck cloth (221).

In the Selenginsk Garrison:
Lower ranks—coat without collar or lapels, green slit cuffs and shoulder strap; yellow buttonhole loops on the sleeves, with small tassels; straw-colored waistcoat and breeches; yellow buttons; black neck cloth; straw-colored back piece on the grenadier cap, with white trim, and dark-green band; drum hoops dark-green with green. Officers—gold buttonhole loops on the sleeves, with metallic thread and small tassels; black neck cloth; hat with toothed wide galloon and a cockcade (Illus. 1084) (222).

In the Irkutsk Garrison:
Lower ranks—coat with puce collar, lapels, cuffs, and shoulder strap; white buttonhole loops on the sleeves, without small tassels, with a puce stripe; straw-colored waistcoat and breeches; white buttons; red neck cloth; drum hoops dark-green with puce. Officers—silver buttonhole loops, without small tassels, with a puce stripe; white neck cloth. For all ranks the same uniform clothing as in the Tobolsk garrison (Illus. 1084) (223).

In the Baltic Garrison:
Lower ranks—coat without collar or lapels, turquoise cuffs and shoulder strap; yellow buttonhole loops on the sleeves, without small tassels; straw-colored waistcoat and breeches; yellow buttons; red neck cloth; drum hoops dark-green with turquoise. Officers—gold buttonhole loops on the sleeves, with metallic thread; white neck cloth (Illus. 1085) (224).

In the Dünamünde Garrison:
Lower ranks—coat without collar or lapels, orange cuffs and shoulder strap; yellow buttonhole loops on the sleeves, with small tassels; straw-colored waistcoat and breeches; yellow buttons; red neck cloth; drum hoops dark-green with orange. Officers—gold buttonhole loops on the sleeves, with small tassels, without metallic thread; white neck cloth (Illus. 1085) (225).

In the Kronstadt Garrison:
Lower ranks—coat without buttonhole loops, with straw-colored collar, lapels, cuffs and, shoulder strap; dark-green waistcoat and breeches; white buttons; red neck cloth (Illus. 1086); sky-blue back piece on the grenadier cap, trim white with black, and a dark-green band; drum hoops dark-green with white. Officers—white neck cloth (Illus. 1086) (226).

In the Narva Garrison:
Lower ranks—coat without buttonhole loops, with red collar, lapels, cuffs, and shoulder strap; dark-green waistcoat and breeches; white buttons; red neck cloth (Illus. 1087). Officers—white neck cloth (227).

In the Yelisavetgrad Garrison, and from 16 December 1798 also in the Kherson Garrison: Lower ranks—coat without buttonhole loops, with camel-colored (verblyuzhii) collar, lapels, cuffs, and shoulder strap; dark-green waistcoat and breeches; yellow buttons; red neck cloth (Illus. 1088). Officers—white neck cloth (228).

In the Dimitrii Garrison:
Lower ranks—coat without buttonhole loops, with white collar, lapels, cuffs, and shoulder strap; dark-green waistcoat and breeches; white buttons; red neck cloth (Illus. 1088). Officers—white neck cloth (229).

In the Azov Garrison:
Lower ranks—coat with pale pink (blednorozovyi) collar, lapels, cuffs, and shoulder strap; dark-green waistcoat and breeches; white buttons; black neck cloth (Illus. 1088). Officers—black neck cloth (230).

In the Omsk Garrison:
Lower ranks—coat without buttonhole loops, with raspberry collar, lapels, cuffs, and shoulder strap; dark-green waistcoat and breeches; white buttons; black neck cloth (Illus. 1089). Officers—black neck cloth (231).

In the Astrakhan Garrison:
Lower ranks—coat without collar, lapels, or buttonhole loops, sand-colored (pesochnyi) cuffs and shoulder strap; dark-green waistcoat and breeches; white buttons; black neck cloth (Illus. 1090). Officers—black neck cloth (232).

In the Tsaritsyn Garrison:
Lower ranks—coat without collar, lapels, or buttonhole loops, with yellow cuffs and shoulder strap; dark-green waistcoat and breeches; yellow buttons; red neck cloth (Illus. 1090). Officers—white neck cloth (233).

In the Kizlyar Garrison:
Lower ranks—coat without collar or buttonhole loops, with red lapels, cuffs, and shoulder strap; dark-green waistcoat and breeches; yellow buttons; black neck cloth (Illus. 1090). Officers—black neck cloth (234).

In the Schlüsselburg Garrison:
Lower ranks— coat without cuff flaps or buttonhole loops, with black collar, lapels, slit cuffs, and shoulder strap; dark-green waistcoat and breeches; yellow buttons, including two in the slit of the cuff and three above; black neck cloth. Officers—black neck cloth (Illus. 1091) (235).

In the Villmanstrand Garrison:
Lower ranks—coat without collar, lapels, or buttonhole loops, with red cuffs and shoulder strap; dark-green waistcoat and breeches; yellow buttons; black neck cloth (Illus. 1090). Officers—white neck cloth (Illus. 1091) (236).

In the Kexholm Garrison:
Lower ranks—coat without lapels or buttonhole loops, with puce collar, cuffs, and shoulder strap; dark-green waistcoat and breeches; white buttons; red neck cloth. Officers—white neck cloth (Illus. 1091) (237).

In the Nyslott Garrison:
Lower ranks—coat without buttonhole loops, with turquoise collar, lapels, cuffs, and shoulder strap; dark-green waistcoat and breeches; yellow buttons; red neck cloth. Officers—white neck cloth (Illus. 1092) (238).

In the Arensburg Garrison:
Lower ranks—coat without lapels or buttonhole loops, with dark-blue (sinii) collar, cuffs, and shoulder strap; dark-green waistcoat and breeches; yellow buttons; red neck cloth. Officers—white

neck cloth (Illus. 1092) (239).

In the Pernau Garrison:
Lower ranks—coat without collar or buttonhole loops, with coffee (kofeinyi) lapels, cuffs, and shoulder strap; dark-green waistcoat and breeches; white buttons; red neck cloth. Officers—white neck cloth (Illus. 1092) (240).

In the Bakhmut Garrison:
Lower ranks—coat without collar, lapels, or buttonhole loops, with light-violet (svetlo-fioletovyi) cuffs and shoulder strap; dark-green waistcoat and breeches; white buttons; black neck cloth. Officers—black neck cloth (Illus. 1093) (241).

In the Tambov Garrison:
Lower ranks—coat without lapels or buttonhole loops, with red collar, cuffs, and shoulder strap; dark-green waistcoat and breeches; yellow buttons; red neck cloth. Officers—white neck cloth (Illus. 1093) (242).

In the Voronezh Garrison:
Lower ranks—coat without lapels or buttonhole loops, with white collar, cuffs, and shoulder strap; dark-green waistcoat and breeches; yellow buttons; red neck cloth. Officers—white neck cloth (Illus. 1093) (243).

In the Vladimir Garrison:
Lower ranks—coat without buttonhole loops, with gray collar, cuffs, lapels, and shoulder strap; dark-green waistcoat and breeches; yellow buttons; red neck cloth (Illus. 1094). Officers—coat without buttonhole loops; white neck cloth (244).

In the Simbirsk Garrison:
Lower ranks—coat without collar or buttonhole loops, with white lapels, cuffs, and shoulder strap; dark-green waistcoat and breeches; white buttons; black neck cloth (Illus. 1095). Officers—black neck cloth (245).

In the Nizhnii-Novgorod Garrison:
Lower ranks—coat without buttonhole loops, with black collar, lapels, cuffs, and shoulder strap: dark-green waistcoat and breeches; white buttons; red neck cloth (Illus. 1096). Officers—white neck cloth (247).

In the Novgorod Garrison:
Lower ranks—coat without lapels or buttonhole loops, with straw-colored collar, cuffs, and shoulder strap; dark-green waistcoat and breeches; yellow buttons; red neck cloth. Officers—white neck cloth (Illus. 1097) (247).

In the Tver Garrison:
Lower ranks—coat without buttonhole loops, with yellow collar, lapels, cuffs, and shoulder strap; dark-green waistcoat and breeches; white buttons; black neck cloth (Illus. 1098). Officers—black neck cloth (248).

In the Aleksandrovsk Garrison:
Lower ranks—coat without buttonhole loops, with chestnut (kashtanovago sveta) collar, lapels, cuffs, and shoulder strap; dark-green waistcoat and breeches; white buttons; black neck cloth (Illus. 1099). Officers—black neck cloth (249).

In the Kirilov, later the former Sudakov, Garrison:
Lower ranks—coat without buttonhole loops, with pink (rozovyi) collar, lapels, cuffs, and shoulder strap; dark-green waistcoat and breeches; white buttons; black neck cloth (Illus. 1100). Officers—black neck cloth (250).

In the Petrovsk Garrison:
Lower ranks—coat without buttonhole loops, with dark-green collar, lapels, cuffs, and shoulder strap; dark-green waistcoat and breeches; white buttons; black neck cloth (Illus. 1100). Officers—black neck cloth (251).

In the Nikitinsk, later the former Balaklava, Garrison, which still later was transferred to the Corfu fortress:
Lower ranks—coat without buttonhole loops, with sand-colored (pesochnyi) collar, lapels, cuffs, and shoulder strap; dark-green waistcoat and breeches; white buttons; black neck cloth (Illus. 1100). Officers—black neck cloth (252).

In the Perekop Garrison:
Lower ranks—coat without lapels or buttonhole loops, with chestnut collar, cuffs, and shoulder strap; dark-green waistcoat and breeches; yellow buttons; black neck cloth (Illus. 1101). Officers—black neck cloth (253).

In the Stavropol Garrison:
Lower ranks—coat without lapels or buttonhole loops, with yellow collar, cuffs, and shoulder strap; dark-green waistcoat and breeches; yellow buttons; black neck cloth (Illus. 1102). Officers—black neck cloth (254).

In the Ozernaya, later the former Orsk, Garrison:
Lower ranks—coat without collar, lapels, or buttonhole loops, with puce cuffs and shoulder strap; dark-green waistcoat and breeches; yellow buttons; black neck cloth (Illus. 1103). Officers—black neck cloth (255).

In the Kizilsk Garrison:
Lower ranks—coat without collar, lapels, or buttonhole loops, with straw-colored cuffs and shoulder strap; dark-green waistcoat and breeches; yellow buttons; black neck cloth (Illus. 1103). Officers—black neck cloth (256).

In the Verkhneuralsk Garrison:
Lower ranks—coat without buttonhole loops, with puce collar, lapels, cuffs, and shoulder strap; dark-green waistcoat and breeches; white buttons; black neck cloth (Illus. 1103). Officers—black neck cloth (257).

In the Troitsk Garrison:
Lower ranks—coat without collar, lapels, or buttonhole loops, with white cuffs and shoulder strap; dark-green waistcoat and breeches; yellow buttons; black neck cloth (Illus. 1104). Officers—black neck cloth (258).

In the Zverinogolovsk Garrison:
Lower ranks—coat without buttonhole loops, with light-green collar, lapels, cuffs, and shoulder strap; dark-green waistcoat and breeches; white buttons; black neck cloth (Illus. 1104). Officers—black neck cloth (259).

In the Senno, later the former Pskov, Garrison:

Lower ranks—coat without lapels or buttonhole loops, with light iron-colored (svetlo-zheleznyi) collar, cuffs, and shoulder strap; dark-green waistcoat and breeches; yellow buttons; red neck cloth (Illus. 1105). Officers—white neck cloth (260).

In the Dünaburg Garrison:

Lower ranks—coat without lapels or buttonhole loops, with orange (oranzhevyi) collar, cuffs, and shoulder strap; dark-green waistcoat and breeches; yellow buttons; red neck cloth (Illus. 1105). Officers—white neck cloth (261).

In the VitebskGarrison:

Lower ranks—coat without collar, lapels, or buttonhole loops, with ruby-colored (yakhontovyi) cuffs and shoulder strap; dark-green waistcoat and breeches; white buttons; red neck cloth (Illus. 1106). Officers—white neck cloth (262).

In the PolotskGarrison:

Lower ranks—coat without buttonhole loops, with puce collar, lapels, cuffs, and shoulder strap; dark-green waistcoat and breeches; yellow buttons; red neck cloth. Officers—white neck cloth (Illus. 1106) (263).

In the Mogilev, later the former Rogachev, Garrison:

Lower ranks—coat without collar or buttonhole loops, with ruby-colored lapels, cuffs, and shoulder strap; dark-green waistcoat and breeches; yellow buttons; black neck cloth (Illus. 1107). Officers—black neck cloth (264).

In the Staryi-Bykhov Garrison:

Lower ranks—coat without buttonhole loops, with light iron-colored collar, lapels, cuffs, and shoulder strap; dark-green waistcoat and breeches; white buttons; red neck cloth (Illus. 1107). Officers—white neck cloth (265).

In the Tomsk Garrison:

Lower ranks—coat without collar or lapels, with gray (dikii) cuffs and shoulder strap; yellow buttons; black neck cloth. Officers—black neck cloth (Illus. 1108) (266).

In the Semipalatinsk Garrison:

Lower ranks—coat without lapels, with apricot (abrikosovyi) collar, cuffs, and shoulder strap; yellow buttons; black neck cloth (Illus. 1109). Officers—black neck cloth (267).

In the Biisk Garrison:

Lower ranks—coat without buttonhole loops, with dark-blue (sinii) collar, lapels, cuffs, and shoulder strap; dark-green waistcoat and breeches; white buttons; black neck cloth. Officers—black neck cloth (Illus. 1110) (268).

In the Petropavlovsk Garrison:

Lower ranks—coat without collar, lapels, or buttonhole loops, with dark-blue (sinii) cuffs and shoulder strap; dark-green waistcoat and breeches. (No information provided on buttons or neck cloth – M.C.) Officers—black neck cloth (Illus. 1110) (269).

In the Mozdok Garrison:

Lower ranks—coat without collar, lapels, or buttonhole loops, with chestnut cuffs and shoulder strap; dark-green waistcoat and breeches; white buttons; black neck cloth (Illus. 1111). Officers—black neck cloth (270).

In the Saratov Garrison:
Lower ranks—coat without collar or buttonhole loops, with straw-colored lapels, cuffs, and shoulder strap; dark-green waistcoat and breeches; yellow buttons; red neck cloth (Illus. 1112). Officers—white neck cloth (271).
In all garrisons beginning with the Kronstadt, drum hoops were dark green with white.

30 September 1797 – Garrison officers were ordered to only have sashes and spontoons when in formation, and not have gorgets. All Garrisons on the internal establishment with dark-green waistcoats and breeches were to wear black baize (baikovyi) neck cloths, without trim (272).
In the Garrison regiments established on a field establishment on 5 January 1798—Rochensalm (Bolotnikov's), Sevastopol(Chirkov's), and Nikolaev (Prince Vyazemskii's)—uniforms were similar to those of other Garrisons on same establishment, with the following distinctions:
In the Rochensalm Garrison:
Lower ranks—coat without lapels, with violet collar, slit cuffs, and shoulder strap; white buttonhole loops on the sleeves, with small tassels; white waistcoat and breeches; white buttons, including two in the slit of each cuff; red neck cloth; white back pieces on the grenadier caps, the caps being trimmed orange with dark green, with orange bands (Illus. 1113). Officers—silver embroidered buttonhole loops, with small tassels; white neck cloth (Illus. 1113) (273).
In the Sevastopol Garrison:
Lower ranks—coat without lapels, with violet collar, cuffs, and shoulder strap; yellow buttonhole loops on the sleeves, with small tassels; white waistcoat and breeches; yellow buttons; red neck cloth; white back pieces on the grenadier caps, the caps being trimmed red with dark green, with red bands (Illus. 1114). Officers—gold embroidered buttonhole loops, with small tassels; white neck cloth (Illus. 1114) (274).
In the Nikolaev Garrison:
Lower ranks—coat without collar, with white lapels, slit cuffs, and shoulder strap; buttonhole loops on the sleeves—white with a mix of the color pink, with small tassels; white waistcoat and breeches; white buttons, including two in the slit of each cuff; red neck cloth (Illus. 1115); red back pieces on the grenadier caps, the caps being trimmed white, with dark-blue bands. Officers—silver embroidered buttonhole loops, with a mix of pink color, with small tassels; white neck cloth (Illus. 1115) (275).

In all three Garrisons drum hoops were dark green with white.

In the Garrisons reclassified on **5 January 1798** from an internal to a field establishment, grenadier caps were of the following colors:

In the Narva Garrison—red back pieces and bands; white trim (276).

In the Omsk Garrison—raspberry back pieces; white trim; dark-green bands (277).

In the Kizlyar Garrison—red back pieces; white trim; yellow bands; (278).

In the Schlüsselburg Garrison—apple-green back pieces; yellow trim; dark-green bands (279).

In the Villmanstrand Garrison—white back pieces; orange trim (no information on bands – M.C.) (280).

In the Kexholm Garrison—light-green back pieces and bands; white trim (281).

In the Nyslott Garrison—sky-blue back pieces and bands; white trime (282).

In the Arensburg Garrison—straw-colored back pieces; white trim; pink bands (283).

In the Pernau Garrison—sky-blue back pieces; white trim; dark-green bands (284).

In the Perekop Garrison—orange back pieces and bands; white trim (285).

In the Orsk Garrison—light-green back pieces; white trim and bands (286).

In the Kizilsk Garrison—straw-colored back pieces; white trim; dark-green bands (287).

In the Verkhneuralsk Garrison—raspberry back pieces; white trim; orange bands (288).

In the Troitsk Garrison—white back pieces; trim yellow with black; sky-blue bands (289).

In the Zverinogolovsk Garrison—light-green back pieces; white trim; orange bands (290).

In the Dünaburg Garrison—orange back pieces; white trim and bands (291).

In the Tomsk Garrison—raspberry back pieces; trim yellow with black; dark-green bands (292).

In the Semipalatinsk Garrison—orange back pieces and bands; white trim (293).

In the Biisk Garrison—dark-blue (temnosinii) back pieces and bands; white trim (294).

In the Petropavlovsk Garrison—red back pieces; white trim; dark-blue (sinii) bands (295).

In the Mozdok Garrison—dark-blue (temnosinii) back pieces; white trim; red bands (296).

In the St.-Petersburg, Viborg, Fredrikshamn, Reval, Kazan, Smolensk, Taganrog, Ikrutsk, Baltic, and Dünamünde Garrisons, which although already existing on a field establishment only had Grenadier companies established by the confirmation of organization tables on 5 January 1798, the colors for grenadier caps were as follows:

In the St.-Petersburg Garrison—white back pieces; trim yellow with black; dark-green bands (297).

In the Viborg Garrison—dark-green back pieces; white trim and bands (298).

In the Fredrikshamn Garrison—dark-green back pieces; white trim; red bands (299).

In the Reval Garrison—white back pieces; trim yellow with black; turquoise bands (300).

In the Kazan Garrison—light-green back pieces; white trim; dark-green bands (301).

In the Smolensk Garrison—black back pieces; white trim; red bands (302).

In the Taganrog Garrison—red back pieces and bands; black trim (303).

In the Irkutsk Garrison—straw-colored back pieces and bands; white trim (304).

In the Baltic Garrison—dark-green back pieces; white trim; straw-colored bands (305).

In the Dünamünde Garrison—straw-colored back pieces; white trim; orange bands (306).

Along with this, i.e. on 5 January 1798, the changes in uniform clothing, weapons, and accouterments for Grenadier and Musketeer regiments also were extended to Garrisons. Consequently, the shafts of halbards and spontoons, and drum sticks, were prescribed to be of the following colors:

In the St.-Petersburg Garrison — coffee.
    — Moscow — white.
    — Viborg — straw-colored.
    — Fredrikshamn — white.
    — Reval — straw-colored.
    — Riga — black.
    — Archangel — black.
    — Kazan — black.
    — Orenburg — black.
    — Smolensk — white.
    — Kiev — straw-colored.
    — Taganrog — straw-colored.
    — Tobolsk — coffee.
    — Selenginsk — straw-colored.
    — Irkutsk — black.
    — Baltic — coffee.
    — Dünamünde — white.
    — Kronstadt — coffee.
    — Narva — white.
    — Yelizavetgrad — white.
    — Dimitrii — straw-colored.
    — Azov — black.
    — Omsk — white.
    — Astrakhan — black.
    — Tsaritsyn — white.
    — Kizlyar — straw-colored.
    — Schlüsselburg — black.
    — Villmanstrand — coffee.
    — Kexholm — coffee.
    — Nyslott — straw-colored
    — Arensburg — black.
    — Pernau — coffee.
    — Bakhmut — straw-colored.
    — Tambov — straw-colored.
    — Voronezh — straw-colored.
    — Vladimir — coffee.
    — Simbirsk — black.
    — Nizhnii-Novgorod — white.
    — Novgorod — white
    — Tver — black

- Aleksandrovsk — black.
- Kirilov — white.
- Petrovsk — white.
- Nikitinsk — straw-colored.
- Perekop — black.
- Stavropol — coffee.
- Orsk — straw-colored.
- Kizilsk — white.
- Verkhneuralsk — white
- Troitsk — black
- Zverinogolovsk — black.
- Senno — black.
- Dünaburg — straw-colored.
- Vitebsk — straw-colored.
- Polotsk — white.
- Mogilev — white.
- Staryi-Bykhov — black.
- Tomsk — coffee.
- Semipalatinsk — black
- Biisk — white
- Petropavlovsk — straw-colored.
- Mozdok — black.
- Saratov — straw-colored.
- Rochensalm — coffee.
- Sevastopol — white.
- Nikolaev — white (307).

In the Nizhne-Kamchatka (Somov's) regiment, established on 3 October 1798, lower ranks had: dark-green coat with puce collar, lapels, cuffs, and shoulder strap; white buttonhole loops on the sleeves, without small tassels; straw-colored waistcoat and breeches; white buttons; red neck cloth; hat with trim (Illus. 1116), and for officers—silver buttonhole loops without small tassels; white neck cloth. In this regiment drum hoops were dark green with white, and non-commissioned officers' halberd and officers' spontoons were white (308).

31 January 1799- The white cloaks established by the table of 5 January 1798 were replaced with dark-green greatcoats (309).

9 October 1799 - The knots (shishki) on officers' sashes, sword knots, and hat tassels, and on lower ranks' sword knots, were ordered to be colored raspberry, and stripes and tassels were to have three colors: black, orange, and raspberry (310).

4 March 1800 – With the disbanding of Grenadier companies in the Viborg, Fredrikshamn, Reval, Riga, Kazan, Orenburg, Smolensk, Kiev, Taganrog, Irkutsk, Dünamünde, Narva, Astrakhan, Schlüsselburg, Villmanstrand, Kexholm, Nyslott, Arensburg, Pernau, Perekop, Orsk, Kizilsk, Verkhneuralsk, Sevastopol, and Nikolaev Garrisons—grenadier caps in these Garrisons are withdrawn. Afterwards, caps remained only in the Grenadier companies of the Archangel,

Kronstadt, Omsk, Tomsk, Selenginsk, Nizhne-Kamchatka, and Gogolev's (in Corfu) Garrisons. The St.-Petersburg Garrison, as already stated, was disbanded.

4 and 9 March 1800 – In Garrisons, waistcoats and breeches were ordered to be only of one color: white. Those that were dark green or straw colored were withdrawn in all cases, as were lower ranks' buttonhole loops on cuffs and trim on hats. All personnel were given black neck cloths. Officers were prescribed the exact same uniforms as lower ranks, except that their hats had narrow galloon (311). Based on these changes, coats in Garrison regiments were as follows:

In Marklovskii 2nd's Regiment (made up of the Narva, Novgorod, Pskov, and Tver Garrisons)— yellow collar, lapels, cuffs, and shoulder strap; white buttons (312); i.e., the same as was for the Tver Garrison.

In Plutalov's Regiment (made up of the Schlüsselburg, Villmanstrand, Kexholm, and Nyslott Garrisons)—black collar, lapels, cuffs, and shoulder strap; yellow buttons (313); i.e., the saem as was for the Schlüsselburg Garrison but with two buttons on the sleeves instead of five.

In Wrangel's Regiment (made up of the Viborg and Fredrikshamn Garrisons)—without collar or lapels, with green cuffs and shoulder strap; white buttons (314); i.e., the same as was for the Viborg Garrison but without buttonhole loops.

In Bolotnikov's Regiment (made up of the Rochensalm and Arensburg Garrisons)—without lapels, with violet collar, cuffs, and shoulder strap; white buttons (315); i.e., the same as was for the Rochensalm Garrison but without buttonhole loops.

In Graf de Castro-Lacerda's Regiment (made up of the Reval and Pernau Garrisons)—without collar or lapels, with turquoise cuffs and shoulder strap; yellow buttons (316); i.e., the same as was for the Reval Garrison but without buttonhole loops.

In Rautenstern's Regiment (made up of the Dünamünde, Smolensk, Vitebsk, and Mogilev Garrisons)—straw-colored collar, lapels, cuffs, and shoulder strap; yellow buttons (317); i.e., the saem as was for the Smolensk Garrison but without buttonhole loops.

In Masse's Regiment (made up of the Kiev and Kherson Garrisons)—without lapels, with red collar, slit cuffs, and shoulder strap; white buttons (318); i.e., the same as was for the Kiev Garrison but without buttonhole loops and, for officers, with narrow gallon on the hat, without zigzags, instead of wide and toothed.

In Prince Vyazemskii's Regiment (made up of the Nikolaev, Perekop, and Sevastopol Garrisons)— without a collar, with white lapels, slit cuffs, shoulder strap, and buttons (319); i.e., the same as was for the Nikolaev Garrison but without buttonhole loops.

In Ol'vintsev's Regiment (made up of the Taganrog, Dimitrii, and Azov garrisons)—with pale pink (blednorozovyi) collar, lapels, cuffs, and shoulder strap; white buttons (320); i.e. the same as was for the Azov Garrison.

In L'vov 1st's Regiment (made up of the Astrakhan, Tsaritsyn, and Simbirsk garrisons)—without collar or lapels, with dark-green cuffs and shoulder strap; white buttons (321); i.e. the same as was in the Astrakhan Regiment but without buttonhole loops.

In Lebedev's Regiment (made up of the Orenburg, Tambov, and Voronezhgarrisons)—without collar or lapesl, with raspberry cuffs and shoulder strap; white buttons (322); i.e. the same as was for the Orenburg Garrison but without buttonhole loops.

In Gogel' 1st's Regiment (made up of the Saratov, Orsk, Zverinogolovsk, and Kizilsk garrisons)—

with light-green collar, lapels, cuffs, and shoulder strap; white buttons (323); i.e. the same as was for the Zverinogolovsk Garrison.

In Lyutov's Regiment (made up of the Semipalatinsk, St.-Peter Fortress, Verkhneuralsk, and Troitsk garrisons)—with puce lapels, cuffs, and shoulder strap; white buttons (324); i.e. similar to what was for the Verkhneuralsk Garrison but without a collar, with slit cuffs instead of round or sewn together, and with four buttons on the sleeves instead of two (Illus. 1117).

In Retyunskii's Regiment (made up of the Omsk, Biisk, Tomsk, and Zhelezinsk garrisons)—with raspberry collar, lapels, cuffs, and shoulder strap; white buttons (325); i.e. the same as was for the Omsk Garrison.

In Leccano's Regiment (made up of the Irkutskand Selenginsk garrisons)—with puce collar, lapels, cuffs, and shoulder strap; white buttons (326); i.e. the same as was for the Tobolsk and Irkutsk garrisons but without buttonhole loops.

In Pushchin 1st's Regiment (made up of the Kazan and Tobolsk garrisons)—with light-green collar, lapels, cuffs, and shoulder strap (327) (no button information provided – M.C.); i.e. the same as was for the Kazangarrison.

In Graf Lieven 1st's Regiment (made up of the Archangel, Vladimir, and Nizhnii-Novgorod garrisons)—with black collar, lapels, cuffs, and shoulder strap; white buttons (328); i.e. the same as was for the Tobolsk garrison but without buttonhole loops.

In Arkharov 2nd's (Moscow)Regiment—with turquoise collar, lapels, and cuffs; yellow buttons (329); i.e. the same as before but without buttonhole loops.

In Bulgakov's (Riga)Regiment—without collar or lapels, with orange cuffs and shoulder strap; yellow buttons (330); i.e. the same as before but without buttonhole loops.

In Ukolov's (Kronstadt)Regiment—with straw-colored collar, lapels, cuffs, and shoulder strap; white buttons (331); i.e. the same as before.

In Somov's (Nizhne-Kamchatka) Regiment—with puce collar, cuffs, and shoulder strap; white buttons (332); i.e. as before but without lapels or buttonhole loops. (Illus. 1118).

There was no special direction regarding Gogolev's Regiment remaining on Corfu, and the new changes were applied only to the Garrisons located within Russia.

In all these regiments beginning with Marklov 2nd's, drum hoops were dark green with white, while drumsticks, as well as non-commissioned officers' halberds and officers' spontoons, kept the colors prescribed by the listing of 5 January 1798 for those Garrisons from which the regiments mentioned here received their uniforms.

28

NOTES

(156) Pattern and various other Foot Artillery uniform clothing items from that time preserved by the Commissariat Department of the War Ministry and in HIS IMPERIAL HIGHNESS GRAND DUKE MICHAEL PAVLOVICH'S Arsenal; drawings of these uniform items held by HIS IMPERIAL MAJESTY'S Own Library; Chronicle of the Russian Imperial Army, compiled by Prince Dolgorukov, Nos. 209, 210, 212, 213, 214, 215, 216, 217, 218, 219, 220, 221, 222, and 223; HIGHEST confirmed table of uniforms, accouterments, and weaponry for Siege and Field Artillery battalions, 12 March 1798, and statements by contemporaries.

(157) Ditto.

(158) Ditto.

(159) Ditto.

(160) Ditto.

(161) Ditto.

(162) The table referenced in the preceding note, and statements by contemporaries.

(163) Ditto.

(164) Ditto.

(165) Pattern and various other Horse Artillery uniform clothing items from that time preserved by the Commissariat Department of the War Ministry and in HIS IMPERIAL HIGHNESS GRAND DUKE MICHAEL PAVLOVICH'S Arsenal; drawings of these uniform items held by HIS IMPERIAL MAJESTY'S Own Library; Chronicle of the Russian Imperial Army, compiled by Prince Dolgorukov, No. 211; HIGHEST confirmed table for a Horse-Artillery battalion, 12 March 1798, and statements by contemporaries.

(166) The table referenced in the preceding note.

(167) Pattern and various other Horse Artillery uniform clothing items from that time preserved by the Commissariat Department of the War Ministry and in HIS IMPERIAL HIGHNESS GRAND DUKE MICHAEL PAVLOVICH'S Arsenal; drawings of these uniform items held by HIS IMPERIAL MAJESTY'S Own Library; HIGHEST confirmed table of uniforms, accouterments, and weapons for a Horse-Artillery battalion, 12 March 1798, and statements by contemporaries.

(168) Ditto.

(169) Ditto.

(170) Ditto.

(171) HIGHEST confirmed table of uniform clothing and accouterment items for the musicians authorized in the senior Siege Artillery battalion, 12 March 1798.

(172) HIGHEST confirmed table of uniform clothing and accouterment items for these commands, 12 March 1798.

(173) HIGHEST confirmed table of uniforms, accouterments, and weapons for a Pioneer regiment, 24 December 1798; drawings of these uniform items held by HIS IMPERIAL MAJESTY'S Own Library, and a model pioneer cap preserved by the Commissariat Department of the War Ministry.

(174) The same table.

(175) The same table and a model sapper cap preserved by the Commissariat Department of the War Ministry.

(176) The same table.

(177) Drawings of uniforms for pioneer officers, held by HIS IMPERIAL MAJESTY'S Own Library.

(178) The table referenced in Note 173, and statements from contemporaries.

(179) HIGHEST confirmed tables of uniform items for sailors of the Baltic and Black-Sea Fleets (1 January 1798), and for the Pontoon command with the Life-Guards Artillery Battalion (10 July 1798); pattern uniform items preserved by the Commissariat Department of the War Ministry; drawings of sailors' uniforms from that time, held by HIS IMPERIAL MAJESTY'S Own Library, including those in the book filed under No. 159, and statements from contemporaries.

(180) Ditto.

(181) Ditto.

(182) Drawings of naval officer uniforms whose patterns were also applicable for pioneer officers, located in book No. 159 as referenced in the preceding note, and statements by contemporaries.

(183) HIGHEST confirmed tables of uniform clothing and other items for Artillery battalions (12 March 1798), the Pioneer regiment (24 December 1798), and the Pontoon command with the Life-Guards Artillery Battalion; also, statements from contemporaries and contemporary drawings.

(184) PSZ Vol. XXV, No. 18,837, pg. 348, and statements by contemporaries.

(185) PSZ, Vol. XLIV, Part II, fourth sect., No. 17,987, pg. 301.

(186) Highest Order.

(187) HIGHEST confirmed table of uniform clothing and other items for the Corps of Engineers, 24 December 1798, and statements from contemporaries.

(188) An ukase signed by the Emperor and announced to the Military Collegium in a report by the Inspector of all Artillery.

(189) PSZ, Vol. XLIV, Part II, fourth sect., under information on uniforms, pg. 3, No. 19,178, and statements by contemporaries.

(190) HIGHEST Directive announced to the State Military Collegium by the TSAREVICHAND GRAND DUKEALEXANDERPAVLOVICH, 20 April 1800.

(191) PSZ, Vol. XXIV, No. 17533, pg. 6; pattern coat preserved by the Commissariat Department of the War Ministry; Chronicle of the Russian Army, compiled by Prince Dolgorukov, No. 89, and this same number in drawings held by HIS IMPERIAL MAJESTY'S Own Library under No. 177.

(192) HIGHEST confirmed table of uniforms, accouterments, and weapons for a single Garrison battalion on the field establishment, 5 January 1798, and pattern garrison uniform clothing preserved by the Commissariat Department of the War Ministry.

(193) The same table, as well as the Military Regulation of 19 November 1796, Pt. X, Chap. V, note to § 8.

(194) The same table.

(195) The same table; drawings held by HIS IMPERIAL MAJESTY'S Own Library under No. 177; Military Regulation of 29 November 1796, Pt. X, Chap. V, note to § 8.

(196) The drawings mentioned in the previous note.

(197) The same drawings and a HIGHEST confirmed table of uniform, accouterments, and weapons for a single Garrison battalion on the internal establishment, 5 January 1798.

(198) The same table and statements by contemporaries.

(199) The same table and a pattern kaftan coat preserved by the Commissariat Department of the War Ministry.

(200) The drawings referenced in Note 195.

(201) Statements from contemporaries.

(202) The table referenced in Note 197.

(203) The same table and PSZ Vol. XLIV, regulations for uniforms, pg. 5, No. 18,122.

(204) The same table.

(205) Ditto.

(206) Statements from contemporaries.

(207) The table referenced in Note 197.

(208) Ditto.

(209) Chronicle of the Russian Imperial Army, compiled by Prince Dolgorukov, No. 89, and under this same number in the drawings located in HIS IMPERIAL MAJESTY'S Own Library under No. 177.

(210) Ibid., No. 94.

(211) Ibid., No. 102.

(212) Ibid., No. 103.

(213) Ibid., No. 109.

(214) Ibid., No. 108.
(215) Ibid., No. 95.
(216) Ibid., No. 138.
(217) Ibid., No. 140.
(218) Ibid., No. 115.
(219) Ibid., No. 121.
(220) Ibid., No. 135.
(221) Ibid., No. 154.
(222) Ibid., No. 148.
(223) Ibid., No. 147.
(224) Ibid., No. 110.
(225) Ibid., No. 111.
(226) Ibid., No. 90.
(227) Ibid., No. 92.
(228) Ibid., No. 122.
(229) Ibid., No. 134.
(230) Ibid., No. 133.
(231) Ibid., No. 149.
(232) Ibid., No. 136.
(233) Ibid., No. 137.
(234) Ibid., No. 132.
(235) Ibid., No. 91.
(236) Ibid., No. 104.
(237) Ibid., No. 105.
(238) Ibid., No. 106.
(239) Ibid., No. 113.
(240) Ibid., No. 112.
(241) Ibid., No. 124.
(242) Ibid., No. 100.
(243) Ibid., No. 99.
(244) Ibid., No. 97.
(245) Ibid., No. 101.
(246) Ibid., No. 98.
(247) Ibid., No. 93.
(248) Ibid., No. 96.
(249) Ibid., No. 125.
(250) Ibid., No. 130.
(251) Ibid., No. 126.
(252) Ibid., No. 129.
(253) Ibid., No. 127.
(254) Ibid., No. 146.
(255) Ibid., No. 141.
(256) Ibid., No. 142.
(257) Ibid., No. 143.
(258) Ibid., No. 144.
(259) Ibid., No. 145.
(260) Ibid., No. 116.
(261) Ibid., No. 114.

(262) Ibid., No. 118.
(263) Ibid., No. 117.
(264) Ibid., No. 119.
(265) Ibid., No. 120.
(266) Ibid., No. 150.
(267) Ibid., No. 151.
(268) Ibid., No. 152.
(269) Ibid., No. 153.
(270) Ibid., No. 131.
(271) Ibid., No. 139.
(272) PSZ, Vol. XXIV, No. 18,173, pg. 754.
(273) Chronicle of the Russian Army, compiled by Prince Dolgorukov, No. 107, and under this same number in the drawings located in HIS IMPERIAL MAJESTY'S Own Library under No. 177.
(274) Ibid., No. 128.
(275) Ibid., No. 123.
(276) Ibid., No. 92.
(277) Ibid., No. 149.
(278) Ibid., No. 132.
(279) Ibid., No. 91.
(280) Ibid., No. 104.
(281) Ibid., No. 105.
(282) Ibid., No. 106.
(283) Ibid., No. 113.
(284) Ibid., No. 112.
(285) Ibid., No. 127.
(286) Ibid., No. 141.
(287) Ibid., No. 142.
(288) Ibid., No. 143.
(289) Ibid., No. 144.
(290) Ibid., No. 145.
(291) Ibid., No. 114.
(292) Ibid., No. 150.
(293) Ibid., No. 151.
(294) Ibid., No. 152.
(295) Ibid., No. 153.
(296) Ibid., No. 131.
(297) Ibid., No. 89.
(298) Ibid., No. 102.
(299) Ibid., No. 103.
(300) Ibid., No. 109.
(301) Ibid., No. 138.
(302) Ibid., No. 115.
(303) Ibid., No. 135.
(304) Ibid., No. 147.
(305) Ibid., No. 110.
(306) Ibid., No. 111.
(307) Ibid., Nos. 89-154.
(308) Drawings of garrison uniforms in 1800, located in HIS IMPERIAL MAJESTY'S Own Library in portfolio

No. 295, and Chronicle of the Russian Imperial Army, compiled by Prince Dolgorukov, No. 155.

(309) PSZ, Vol. XXV, No. 18,837, pg. 548, and statements by contemporaries.

(310) PSZ, Vol. XLIV, Part II, fourth sect., under information on uniforms, pg. 3, No. 19, 178, and statements by contemporaries.

(311) Drawings of garrison uniforms in 1800, located in HIS IMPERIAL MAJESTY'S Own Library in portfolio No. 295, and HIGHEST ORDER, 4 March 1800.

(312) Ditto.

(313) Ditto.

(314) Ditto.

(315) Ditto.

(316) Ditto.

(317) Ditto.

(318) Ditto.

(319) Ditto.

(320) Ditto.

(321) Ditto.

(322) Ditto.

(323) Ditto.

(324) Ditto.

(325) Ditto.

(326) Ditto.

(327) Ditto.

(328) Ditto.

(329) Ditto.

(330) Ditto.

(331) Ditto.

(332) Ditto.

РИСУНКИ
Одежды и Вооруженія
РОССІЙСКИХЪ
ВОЙСКЪ.

PLATES LIST OF ILLUSTRATIONS

1059. Bombardier and Fireworker. Foot Artillery, 1796-1801.

1060. Drummers. Foot Artillery, 1796-1801

1061. Officer. Foot Artillery, 1797-1801.

1062. Junior Train Master (Unter-Furmeister). Field Artillery, 1797-1801.

1063. Bombardier and Fireworker. Horse Artillery, 1797-1801.

1064. Officer. Horse Artillery, 1797-1801.

1065. Musician. Foot Artillery, 1797-1801.

1066. Pioneer, 1797-1801.

1067. Pioneer Cap, 1797-1801.

1068. Pioneers. Non-commissioned Officer and Drummer, 1797-1801.

1069. Sapper, 1797-1801.

1070. Sapper Cap, 1797-1801.

1071. Pioneer Regimental Drummer, 1797-1801.

1072. Company-grade Officer. Pioneer Regiment, 1797-1801.

1073. Pontooneers, 1797-1801.

1074. Pontooneers, 1797-1801. (In working dress.)

1075. Officer and Non-commissioned Officer. Pontoon Depots, 1797-1801.

1076. Engineer Officer, 1800-1801.

1077. Musketeers. St.-Petersburg and Moscow Garrisons, 1796-1800.

1078. Non-commissioned Officers. Viborg and Fredrikshamn Garrisons, 1797-1800.

1079. Musketeer Drummer. Reval Garrison, 1797-1800.

1080. Non-commissioned Officer and Private. Grenadier Companies of the Riga Garrison, 1797-1800.

1081. Fifer and Drummer. Grenadier Companies of the Archangel Garrison, 1797-1801.

1082. Regimental Drummers. Kazan and Orenburg Garrisons, 1797-1800.

1083. Company-grade Officers. Taganrog, Smolensk, and Kiev Garrisons, 1797-1800.

1084. Field-grade Officers. Selenginsk and Tobolsk Garrisons, 1797-1800.

1085. Generals. Baltic and Dünamünde Garrisons, 1797-1800.

1086. Non-commissioned Officer and Officer. Kronstadt Garrison, 1797-1800.

1087. Musketeer. Narva Garrison, 1797-1800.

1088. Non-commissioned Officers. Yelisavetgrad, Dimitrii, and Azov Garrisons, 1797-1800.

1089. Musketeer Drummer. Omsk Garrison, 1797-1800.

1090. Regimental Drummers. Astrakhan, Kizlyar, and Tsaritsyn Garrisons, 1797-1800.

1091. Company-grade Officers. Schlüsselburg, Villmanstrand, and Kexholm Garrisons, 1797-1800.

1092. Field-grade Officers. Nyslott, Pernau, and Arensburg Garrisons, 1797-1800.

1093. Generals. Bakhmut, Tambovsk, and Voronezh Garrisons, 1797-1800.

1094. Musketeer, Vladimir Garrison, 1797-1800. Garrison Invalid, 1797-1801.

1095. Non-commissioned Officers, Simbirsk Garrison, 1797-1801. Invalid Non-commissioned Officer, 1797-1801.

1096. Company Drummers, Nizhnii-Novgorod Garrison, 1797-1800. Invalid Company Drummer, 1797-1801.

1097. Company-grade Officers, Novgorod Garrison, 1797-1800. Invalid Company-grade Officer, 1797-1801.

1098. Musketeer. Tver Garrison, 1797-1800.

1099. Musketeer. Aleksandrovsk Garrison, 1797-1800.

1100. Non-commissioned Officers. Kirilov, Petrovsk, and Nikitinsk Garrisons, 1797-1800.

1101. Musketeer. Perekop Garrison, 1797-1800.

1102. Non-commissioned Officers. Stavropol Garrison, 1797-1800.

1103. Non-commissioned Officers. Orsk, Kizilsk, and Verkhneuralsk Garrisons, 1797-1800.

1104. Non-commissioned Officers. Troitsk and Zverinogolovsk Garrisons, 1797-1800.

1105. Musketeers. Senno and Dünaburg Garrisons, 1797-1800.

1106. Musketeer, Vitebsk Garrison, and Officer, Polotsk Garrison, 1797-1800.

1107. Field-grade Officers. Rogachev and Staryi-Bykhov Garrisons, 1797-1800.

1108. General. Tomsk Garrison, 1797-1800.

1109. Musketeer. Semipalatinsk Garrison, 1797-1800.

1110. Field-grade Officers. Biisk and Petropavlovsk Garrisons, 1797-1800.

1111. Musketeer. Mozdok Garrison, 1797-1800.

1112. Non-commissioned Officer. Saratov Garrison, 1797-1800.

1113. Company-grade Officer and Grenadiers. Rochensalm Garrison, 1798-1800.

1114. Grenadier and Company-grade Officer. Sevastopol Garrison, 1798-1800.

1115. General and Musketeer. Nikolaev Garrison, 1798-1800.

1116. Field-grade Officer and Musketeer. Nizhne-Kamchatka Garrison, 1798-1800.

1117. Musketeer and Field-grade Officer. Semipalatinsk, Petropavlovsk, Verkhneuralsk, and Troitsk Garrisons, 1800-1801.

1118. Non-commissioned Officer. Nizhne-Kamchatka Garrison, 1800-1801.

Bombardier and Fireworker. Foot Artillery, 1796-1801.

Drummers. Foot Artillery, 1797-1801.

Officer. Foot Artillery, 1797-1801.

1062.

Junior Train Master (Unter-Furmeister). Field Artillery, 1797-1801.

Составл. Тубаревъ и Борисовъ.

Вк. на кам. Валоцова и Туря.

Bombardier and Fireworker. Horse Artillery, 1797-1801.

1064.

Составл Пиратский и Тверской.   Рис. на кам. Шмидт и Ференрихт.

Officer. Horse Artillery, 1797-1801.

1065.

Составл. Василенко и Борисовъ.

Рис. на кам. Белоусовъ.

Musician. Foot Artillery, 1797-1801.

Пис. Павл. Клюквинъ. Рис. на кам. Бѣлоусовъ и Гиллеръ.

Pioneer, 1797-1801.

106.

Pioneer Cap, 1797-1801.

Pioneers. Non-commissioned Officer and Drummer, 1797-1801.

Составл. Василченко и Захаровъ.   Рис. накам. Бѣлоусовъ и Турке

Sapper, 1797-1801.

1070.

Sapper Cap, 1797-1801.

1071.

Pioneer Regimental Drummer, 1797-1801.

1072.

Составили Василченко и Вишневецкій.

Рис. на кам. Гурке.

Company-grade Officer. Pioneer Regiment, 1797-1801.

1073.

Pontooneers, 1797-1801

Pontooneers, 1797-1801. (In working dress.)

Officer and Non-commissioned Officer. Pontoon Depots, 1797-1801.

Engineer Officer, 1800-1801.

Составл. Васильченко и. Клюквинъ.   Рис. на кам. Бѣлоусовъ.

Musketeers. St.-Petersburg and Moscow Garrisons, 1796-1800.

Non-commissioned Officers. Viborg and Fredrikshamn Garrisons, 1797-1800.

Составл. Василченко и Берстовъ.

Рис. на кам. Бѣлоусовъ и Юль.

Musketeer Drummer. Reval Garrison, 1797-1800.

1080.

Составл: Впсильенко и Вишневецкий.   Рис. на кам. Жорков.

NCO and Private. Grenadier Companies of the Riga Garrison, 1797-1800.

Fifer and Drummer. Grenadier Companies of the Archangel Garrison, 1797-1801.

Составил Васильченко и Борисова.

Тип. на кам. Гиллерь.

Regimental Drummers. Kazan and Orenburg Garrisons, 1797-1800.

Составъ. Василенко и Разумихинъ.　　　　　　　　Рис. на кам. Кол.

Company-grade Officers. Taganrog, Smolensk, and Kiev Garrisons, 1797-1800.

Составл. Василченко и Берестовъ.

Рис. на кам. Бѣлоусовъ и Ярнлундъ.

Field-grade Officers. Selenginsk and Tobolsk Garrisons, 1797-1800.

1085.

Составл. Василченко и Борисовъ.

Рис. на кам. Гиллерв.

Generals. Baltic and Dünamünde Garrisons, 1797-1800.

Non-commissioned Officer and Officer. Kronstadt Garrison, 1797-1800.

Составл. Васильченко и Радумихинъ.   Рис. на камнѣ Бѣлоусовъ и Киллеръ.

Musketeer. Narva Garrison, 1797-1800.

Non-commissioned Officers. Yelisavetgrad, Dimitrii, and Azov Garrisons, 1797-1800.

Musketeer Drummer. Omsk Garrison, 1797-1800.

Regimental Drummers. Astrakhan, Kizlyar, and Tsaritsyn Garrisons, 1797-1800.

1091.

Company-grade Officers. Schlüsselburg, Villmanstrand, and Kexholm Garrisons, 1797-1800.

Составл. Василченко и Разумихинъ.   Рис. на кам. Гурне.

Field-grade Officers. Nyslott, Pernau, and Arensburg Garrisons, 1797-1800.

1093.

Generals. Bakhmut, Tambovsk, and Voronezh Garrisons, 1797-1800.

1094.

Musketeer, Vladimir Garrison, 1797-1800. Garrison Invalid, 1797-1801.

1095.

NCO Simbirsk Garrison, 1797-1801. Invalid Non-commissioned Officer, 1797-1801.

1096.

Cp. Drummers, Nizhnii-Novgorod Garrison, 1797-1800. Invalid Cp.Drummer, 1797-1801.

Cp-grade Officers, Novgorod Garrison, 1797-1800. Invalid Cp-grade Officer, 1797-1801.

Musketeer. Tver Garrison, 1797-1800.

Составъ Василченко и Раурьшихинз

Рис. на камнѣ Бѣлоусовъ и Гурке

Musketeer. Aleksandrovsk Garrison, 1797-1800.

Non-commissioned Officers. Kirilov, Petrovsk, and Nikitinsk Garrisons, 1797-1800.

Состав. Васильченко и Борисовъ.

Рис. на кам. Белоусовъ и Кизе.

Musketeer. Perekop Garrison, 1797-1800.

Non-commissioned Officers. Stavropol Garrison, 1797-1800.

Non-commissioned Officers. Orsk, Kizilsk, and Verkhneuralsk Garrisons, 1797-1800.

Non-commissioned Officers. Troitsk and Zverinogolovsk Garrisons, 1797-1800.

Musketeers. Senno and Dünaburg Garrisons, 1797-1800.

1106.

Составил Васильченко и Клюквинъ.

Рисовалъ Балдаровъ и Ком.

Musketeer, Vitebsk Garrison, and Officer, Polotsk Garrison, 1797-1800.

1107.

Field-grade Officers. Rogachev and Staryi-Bykhov Garrisons, 1797-1800.

Составл. Васильченко и Вишневский.   Рис. на кам. Белоусовъ и Жарновъ.

General. Tomsk Garrison, 1797-1800.

Musketeer. Semipalatinsk Garrison, 1797-1800.

Составл. Васильченко и Разумихинъ.　Рис. на кам. Бѣлоусовъ и Гольдр.

Field-grade Officers. Biisk and Petropavlovsk Garrisons, 1797-1800.

Musketeer. Mozdok Garrison, 1797-1800.

Non-commissioned Officer. Saratov Garrison, 1797-1800.

Company-grade Officer and Grenadiers. Rochensalm Garrison, 1798-1800.

Grenadier and Company-grade Officer. Sevastopol Garrison, 1798-1800.

General and Musketeer. Nikolaev Garrison, 1798-1800.

Field-grade Officer and Musketeer. Nizhne-Kamchatka Garrison, 1798-1800.

1117.

Musketeer and Officer. Semipalatinsk, Petropavlovsk, and Troitsk Garrisons, 1800-1801.

Составл. Василченко и Берестов.   Рис. на кам. Белоусов и Турне.

Non-commissioned Officer. Nizhne-Kamchatka Garrison, 1800-1801.

WORK PLAN

Our reprint in based on the original 19th century volumes, to be precise the volumes from 7 to 9 are dedicated to the reign of Paul I; this first part is distributed on 7 volumes, having a numbering from 1 to 7. From number 10 to 18 of the original volumes, the second part is dedicated to the Russian troops under Alexander I. These still being worked on and they will be soon ready, distributed on twenty volumes approximately. Our new edition, the first ever published in English, both on paper and digital format, boasts a large number of color plates, many of them unpublished and coloured by our team of expert artists and scholars of uniformology. Each volume is based on 50/70 plates, always accompanied by the original translated text which describes the uniforms, the organization and the armament of the Russian army of the period.

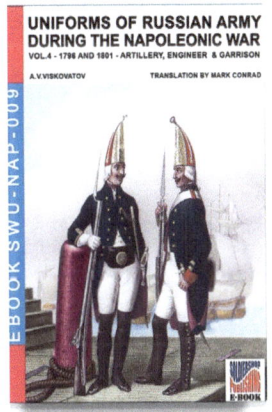

www.ingramcontent.com/pod-product-compliance
Lightning Source LLC
Chambersburg PA
CBHW041456120626

46547CB00003B/453